W9-CTV-137

THE BASICS OF
WINNING
BLACKJACK

J. Edward Allen

- Gambling Research Institute -
Cardoza Publishing

Cardoza Publishing, publisher of **Gambling Research Institute** (GRI) books, is the foremost gaming and gambling publisher in the world with a library of more than 50 up-to-date and easy-to-read books and strategies. These authoritative works are written by the top experts in their fields and with more than 5,000,000 books in print, represent the best-selling and most popular gaming books anywhere.

Printing History

First Printing	October 1984
Second Printing	February 1985
Third Printing	September 1986
Fourth Printing	September 1987
Fifth Printing	October 1988
Sixth Printing	March 1990

New Revised Edition

First Printing	August 1992
Second Printing	August 1993
Third Printing	March 1995

Copyright © 1984, 1992 by Gambling Research Institute
- All Rights Reserved -

ISBN:0-940685-24-8
Library of Congress Catalogue Card Number: 92-72054
Special thanks to Ed and Linda Weinstein of Marion & Co., for generous use of casino gaming props for cover photo.
Cover Photo by Ron Charles

Write for your free catalogue of gambling books, advanced and computer strategies.

CARDOZA PUBLISHING
P.O. Box 1500, Cooper Station, New York, NY 10276
Phone (718)743-5229 • Fax (718)743-8284

Table of Contents

Illustrations and Charts

Illustrations

Charts

I. Introduction

Blackjack's popularity continues to grow for it's the only game in the casino where the player has an edge over the house. This newly revised edition shows you how to take advantage of that edge and beat any game the casino offers, whether it's single or multiple deck blackjack!

In order to have this edge, the player must know basic strategy and play this strategy correctly. But that's not difficult to do, and it's all here in this guide - everything the player must know to play at his best and beat the house.

The strategies shown in this book are based upon computer studies and should be studied carefully. They're explained so that anyone, after a few hours or less of practice, can be a winner at blackjack.

The book is written in simple and clear language, and its one purpose is in making you, the reader, a winner at this most popular and exciting casino game!

II. The Blackjack Scene

The area devoted to blackjack in any casino will usually be the largest area devoted to any of the table games, which include not only blackjack, but craps, roulette and baccarat. In fact, in many casinos the game is so popular that several areas may offer the game of blackjack.

It's therefore not hard to find a game when entering the casino. There will be a number of tables placed so that they surround a center area from which the casino personnel operate. This is known as the **blackjack pit**.

The Table

The blackjack table is a modified oval, with the seats arranged around the curved portion. There will be as many seats available as spots on the table.

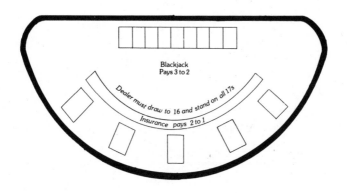

Blackjack
Pays 3 to 2

Dealer must draw to 16 and stand on all 17s

Insurance pays 2 to 1

The number of seats available at a blackjack table ranges from five to seven depending upon the casino. While the players remain seated throughout the game (unless they wish to stand) the dealer stands and faces them from the inside of the pit.

Directly in front of the dealer is the chip rack, containing the casino chips. To his right (sometimes to his left) is a slot where cash is dropped when players come to the table and change cash for chips.

Also on the table may be a **shoe** which is a rectangular box, either made of plastic or wood, which holds at least four decks of cards. If the game is played with only one or two decks, there will be no shoe on the table.

There may also be a small sign stating the minimum bet (and sometimes the maximum one) permitted at the table. Sometimes this small sign shows additional rules, other than those imprinted on the green felt covering the table.

The green felt contains boxes where each player will place his chips for betting purposes, and where usually two or three rules of the game are printed. The most common is *Dealer Must Draw to 16, and Stand on All 17s*, which refers to the totals of the points the dealer holds. The next most common rule is *Insurance Pays 2-1*. The third is *Blackjack Pays 3-2*.

These are very basic rules that we need not concern ourselves with right now, for they will be fully explained at the appropriate time.

The Dealer

Unlike the players, the dealer stands throughout the game, and wears the house uniform. In these days of tighter security, there is usually some name tag and sometimes a picture of the dealer attached, so that the players can, by looking closely, ascertain the name of the dealer.

The dealer runs the game. He changes cash into chips issued by the casino; he **changes color**—that is, changing casino chips into smaller or larger denominations. He shuffles the cards, and deals them

8

out. He pays off winning bets and collects losing bets. He answers questions of the players, and is there to help them, as well as run the game.

Tipping the Dealer

Tipping, or **toking** the dealer, to use a casino term, is not required, but is often done. Some players overtip; others never tip at all. And some, if they tip, don't do it correctly.

A dealer should be toked if you feel that he or she has been friendly and helpful, and has made your game more enjoyable. In that case, every now and then you can make a bet for the dealer by putting out a chip above your box in the area marked for insurance bets.

When you do this, if you win your bet, the dealer will win his; if you lose, the dealer will also lose. The dealers prefer this kind of toking, for it gives them the chance to double the original bet, and sometimes win even more if the player is dealt a blackjack.

Sometimes players tip after a blackjack is dealt to them, but one must remember that no matter how generous you want to be, your edge at blackjack is very slight, and overtipping will erode your winnings. Strike a happy balance, but under no circumstances tip a hostile or unfriendly dealer, or one who wants you to lose and considers you a sucker for playing.

The Casino Chips

Casino personnel call chips **checks**, but we're going to use the term chips throughout this book because it's the most popular term, understood by all players.

These are issued by a casino in standard denominations; usually for $1, $5, $25, and $100. Some casinos have $500 and even higher denomination chips, and many casinos have 50¢ chips at the blackjack table, because payoffs are often in this amount. There are casinos that don't bother issuing chips this small, and instead pay off with coins, either half-dollars or quarters. In some of the Northern Nevada casinos, $2.50 chips are used at the blackjack tables, saving the dealers time and trouble when payoffs for $5 blackjacks are made. A blackjack, which will be explained later, pays 3-2, and a $5 wager will be paid off with $7.50.

Players can also play with cash, but casino executives frown on this. Some players like to play only in cash, but if they win they'll have to settle for casino chips as their payoff. Dealers will always pay off in casino chips, not in cash.

Casinos have minimum betting limits, which usually are $1 or $2. Some tables may have $5 or $25 or even higher minimum limits, because *high rollers* don't want to be betting thousands while some other player is betting $2 at a time.

After you leave a table, you can cash in your casino chips at the **cashier's cage** of the casino. If you don't spot it, any security guard or other casino personnel will show you where it is. That's where you get cash for your chips, not at the blackjack table.

The Players

Even though there may be five to seven spots open for players at any blackjack table, the game will begin if one player shows up to play. When more than one player is at a table, additional players can take any of the vacant seats. There is no set rule where one is to sit.

The cards are dealt, as we shall see, in a clockwise fashion so that the player to the dealer's left, facing him, is the first player to receive cards. He is known as the **first baseman**. The player at the other end of the table, nearest to the dealer's right, is the last player to receive cards, and he's known as the **third baseman** or **anchorman.**

Where should one sit at a table if given the choice? Most experts prefer either the third baseman's seat or the one to its right, for they get a look at the other hands before they have to make any playing decisions.

But if you're a beginner, don't sit in the third baseman's seat. You might feel too much pressure, for sometimes when you draw a card you'll inadvertently make the dealer a winner. Even though you made the right decision, ignorant players may unfairly blame you for their losses. But, as you get more expert, sit as close to the third baseman's seat as you can, for you get that little extra information playing last.

Players in casino blackjack play their hands as individuals, trying to beat the dealer, not each other. When you are dealt cards, all you want to do is get a better hand than the dealer, so you can win. The other hands are immaterial to this result, and often some players at the table will win a hand while others will be losing their hands.

III. The Cards and Rules of Play

The Cards

A standard deck of 52 cards is used in the game of casino blackjack. At one time most games were played with this single deck of cards, but today there are many multiple deck games in existence. But no matter how many decks are used, whether two or eight, they are merely multiples of the standard 52 deck game. Therefore, if a player is at a table where two decks are used, the dealer is using 104 cards, made up of two standard decks of 52 cards each.

The standard deck of cards contains four suits; clubs, diamonds, hearts and spades. In blackjack, the suits have no material value and can be disregarded. What is important is the value of the cards.

Value of the Cards

Each of the four suits contains the identical 13

cards, ranging from an ace to a king. The cards are ace, 2, 3, 4, 5, 6, 7, 8, 9, 10, jack, queen and king.

In casino blackjack, the following cards are counted as 10s, and have that value for adding purposes to ascertain the total of the hand: 10, jack, queen and king.

In the future, we'll refer to any of these cards as a **10-value card** or simply as a **10.** There are sixteen 10-value cards in the standard deck, and therefore these are the most frequent cards in play. All the other values consist of only four cards.

To value a card, other than the ace, which we'll write about last, we simply examine the spots on the card, as well as the numerical value in the form of a number at the corners. Thus a 2 has two spots, the 3 three, the 4 four, and all the way up to the 9, which has 9 spots.

The ace is the most powerful card in blackjack, and one of the reasons for its importance is that it can be valued, at the option of the player, as either a 1 or 11.

Blackjack is also called **21** because that is the highest total that a player may validly hold. Any hand totaling more than 21 points is a loser, and so called a **"bust."** The ace, which can be valued at 1 or 11, sometimes prevents hands from going over 21, or "busting"—that is, losing, when it is valued as a 1.

For example, a hand containing 10-3-ace is merely a 14, not a 24, because the player simply values the ace as a 1. The ace gives players, especially beginners, the most trouble. Often they think they've busted, or lost, because they value the ace as an 11 instead of as a 1. If in doubt, show the hand to the dealer and let him value it for you.

Object of the Game

When we discuss the object of the game, we write about the object from the player's standpoint. The dealer has no object to his play; he simply must follow the rules set forth by the casino, which is to stand on hands of 17 or more, and draw to all hands of 16 or less.

The object of the game, in its most simple terms, is to beat the dealer. To do this, the player can win in two ways. First of all, he or she must have a total higher than the dealer's total, or he or she must have a valid hand, of whatever total, while the dealer "busts" or goes over 21.

The player loses if his or her total is less than the dealer's total, or if the player busts. Once the player busts, his hand is out of play and his bet is removed. It doesn't matter to this player if the dealer subsequently busts his own hand; once the player busts, he loses.

If both the player and the dealer have the same totals in their respective hands, it's a tie, a standoff. The casino term for this is a **"push."** And that's just what it is, a push. Neither the player nor the dealer win.

How does a player improve his total? First, to understand this concept, we have to look at the original hand dealt to the player.

The Original Hand

The dealer, to put a round of play in motion, deals out two cards to each of the players and two cards to himself. The cards are dealt one at a time, face down, the player to the dealer's left getting the first card, and then each player after that getting a card in clockwise fashion. After each player has received one card, then the dealer gives himself a card, also face down. Then a second card is dealt to each of the players, also face down, in the same order, and the dealer gets his second card, and turns it face up.

This face up card is known as the **upcard**. Thus, all the players see one of the dealer's cards, but the dealer sees none of the players' cards. It wouldn't matter if he saw the players' cards or not, for the dealer, as we have said, is bound by strict rules. In some casinos, in multiple deck games, the players' cards are dealt face up.

Most players prefer to have their cards dealt face down, for it gives them a feeling they're actually involved in a secret game of some sort, hiding their cards from the dealer, who couldn't care less. But most experts prefer to see all the cards dealt face up, because they get a better grasp of what cards are in play and out of the deck, and this gives them a slight advantage.

The two cards the player gets at the outset of play is an original hand. The highest total he can get is 21 on on original hand; an ace and a 10-value card. When a player (or dealer) gets this hand, it's known as a **blackjack**, or a **natural**. A blackjack pays 3-2 if it wins. All other winning hands pay even-money. If a dealer gets a blackjack and none of the players have a blackjack, the dealer simply wins the player's bet at even-money; he doesn't get that extra bonus.

If a player and the dealer have a blackjack, then it's a push; neither win.

The next highest total is a 20. This is a very strong hand, and usually a winning one, either on the part of the dealer or the player. Thereafter, the hands go down in value.

The important thing to remember is that neither a player nor a dealer can bust on the original hand. The following are some original hands and their totals:

Hand	Total
queen-5	15
9-8	17
4-8	12
10-king	20
ace-8	19

Hitting and Standing

If a player wants to improve his hand, he can draw a card to that hand. This is called **hitting** or **drawing**. For example, if a player is dealt a 5-3, his total is only 8. Even if he hits the hand, he can't bust, or go over 21. So he hits the hand, not worrying about busting.

If a player is dealt a 10-king, he has a total of 20. He doesn't want to hit this hand, for his total is very strong, just one below the highest possible total, and if he hits the hand he will bust unless he gets an ace, and the odds against getting one of the four aces is very high indeed, so he stands.

Hard and Soft Totals

Any hand that doesn't contain an ace is a **hard** hand, and the total of those hard hands are **hard totals**. Most of the hands dealt to either the player or the dealer will be hard hands like these.

Some examples of hard hands:

5-4, which is a hard 9.
10-5, which is a hard 15.
Jack-king, which is a hard 20.

There is another way to have a hard hand, and that is to have a hand containing an ace, where the ace is counted as 1, not as an 11. For example, suppose the player were dealt an original hand of 10-4, and hit it and got an ace. He now would have hard 15, because he must value the ace as 1. If he valued it as an 11, the hand would total 25 and bust.

Other hard hands containing an ace:

10-6-ace, which is a hard 17.
9-4-ace, which is a hard 14.
8-3-ace, which is a hard 12.

Any hand which contains an ace that is valued at 11, rather than as 1, is a **soft** hand, and its total is a **soft total**.

For example, suppose a player received an original hand of ace-9. It would be a soft 20, with the ace counted as an 11. Of course, the player would have the option of counting the hand a 10, but that would be foolish, since his 20 is very strong, and if he counted it as a 10 and hit the hand, any card drawn other than an ace or ten-value would weaken the hand.

Here are some examples of soft hands:

ace-9 is a soft 20.

ace-8 is a soft 19.

ace-7 is a soft 18.

A soft hand has one important advantage. Even if the hand is hit, it can't bust. So if a foolish player hit a soft 20, consisting of an ace and 9, he still couldn't bust.

A soft hand can become a hard hand, if it's drawn to. For example, if a player were dealt an ace-6 for a soft 17 and hit and got an 8, his hand would now be a hard 15 (ace-6-8 = 15). An ace-4, which is a soft 15, if hit with a 7, would become a hard 12. But the same ace-4, if hit with a 5, would become a soft 20.

We'll go into the strategies of hitting or standing on soft totals later on.

The Blackjack

This is the strongest of all hands, and consists of an ace and a 10-value card (10, jack, queen or king) dealt as an original hand. It is an immediate winner for the player—unless the dealer has a blackjack also, in which case it is a push. But if the dealer doesn't have a blackjack, it pays off at 3-2.

If the dealer has a blackjack and none of the players have one, then the dealer wins all the bets at the table.

As we shall see, the player has an option of splitting aces and playing each ace as a separate hand. If a ten-value card is dealt to a split ace, it's not a blackjack, just a 21.

Remember, only an ace and a 10-value card in the original hand is a blackjack.

Busting

Sometimes this is also known as **breaking**, but busting is the more common term used in casinos. When either a player or a dealer has drawn cards to his or her original hand and gone over 21, the hand is a losing one; for he or she has busted. The only valid hands are those of 21 or fewer points.

When we bust—that is, go over 21 after hitting our hand—we must turn the cards over immediately to show that we lost, and the dealer will, at that point, take away both our cards and our chips. We've lost, and are out of the game for that round of play, even if the dealer subsequently busts. This is the really big edge the casino has over us. If the dealer and the player both bust, the player still loses.

Well, then, you might ask, why would anyone risk drawing and busting a hand? As we shall see, there are times when the dealer's upcard forces us to hit our hand, even though we may bust, because he probably has a 17 or higher total, and if we stand with a **stiff** total, or 12 to 16, we'll lose our bets without even trying to improve our hands.

IV. Playing the Casino Game

We're now ready to see how the game is played in a casino. For purposes of this illustration, we're going to assume we enter a casino to play some 21. The first thing we do is head for the blackjack pit, and look for a table that will accommodate our wagers. If we wish to bet only $2 a hand, we must find a table with a $1 or $2 minimum, and avoid the tables with a $5 or higher minimum.

We find several tables like that, and at one table only two other players are seated, one in the first baseman's spot at the extreme left of the dealer. The other player is in the center spot, so we move to the anchorman's seat and take out some cash, place it on the table, and wait for the dealer to change this into casino chips.

The dealer is about to shuffle up the cards, and so he puts them down and takes our cash. Our involvement with casino blackjack is about to begin.

Changing Cash into Chips

We are already seated in the last chair when the dealer takes our cash and counts it. We had put down $40, in assorted $10s and $20s, and the dealer will turn the money over after counting it, to verify that it's not *funny money* with one denomination printed on the front and a different one printed on the back.

In most casinos, he'll not only verify the amount with us by announcing *forty dollars*, but will try and catch the attention of a casino executive, a floorman, who will be in the interior of the pit, supervising the games. After the floorman acknowledges that this cash amount is being exchanged for chips, the dealer will drop the cash into a slot and it will disappear from view.

Then he'll give us $40 worth of chips. Since it's a $2 table, he might give us $20 worth of $1 chips and four $5 chips. We count the chips after he gives them to us. Anyone can make a mistake, and this is perfectly acceptable behavior.

While we're doing this, the dealer is shuffling the cards.

Shuffling, Cutting and Burning a Card

In the casino we're playing at, there are both one-deck and multiple-deck games, but we've sat at a table with a one-deck game. The dealer is shuffling up the cards, doing a thorough job. When he's finished, the cards are placed on the table in front of one of the players to be cut. Some players, out of superstition, refuse to cut the cards, which is also acceptable. But the player sitting in the first base cuts them by taking up a portion of the cards and placing them next to the original stack of cards. In some casinos, a plastic card is handed to the player to be inserted somewhere in the deck, then the cards on top of the card are placed below it. Either cut is legitimate.

After the cards are cut, the dealer places them all together, and then removes the top card, and either places it on the bottom of the deck, face up (but in such a manner that the players cannot see its value) or takes the top card and places it in a small plastic case to his right, face down. If he does the latter, then all future discards—that is, cards already played out—will be placed atop that card. If he turns the card face up at the bottom of the deck, then all future discards will be placed face up below that burned card.

The above paragraph describes what is meant by **burning a card**. This is a ritual carried out in practically all casinos, and hearkens back to the days when the casino was worried that someone would cut to a precise part of the deck, and thus take advantage of knowledge of the top card. Which still might be done, for all we know.

Making a Bet

As the dealer holds the cards, getting ready to deal, the players make their bets. We will see a rectangular printed box right in front of our seat, and this is where our chips go.

The bet must be made prior to the deal of the cards. It must be at least the minimum allowed at the table, and cannot be more than the maximum permitted at the table.

But we're not thinking of $500 bets (usually the maximum at most casinos) as we put out two $1 chips. We're going to get our feet wet and test the waters that Lady Luck swims in so cunningly. Our chips are now in our betting box, and since the other two players have also made their bets, the dealer is ready to deal out the cards.

The Deal

The first baseman gets the top card, face down, and then the second player gets his card, and we then get ours. The last of the first cards to be dealt goes to the dealer, also face down. Now a second card goes out in the same order, but the dealer turns over this card, his upcard.

We now all have original hands of two cards, and can exercise our various options, or *act upon* our hands. For purposes of this illustration, we're simply going to make a decision as to whether to hit or stand.

Hitting or Standing—How To

To refresh our recollection, hitting means drawing a card to our original hand. We can hit our hand as often as we care to, so long as the total of the cards doesn't exceed 21.

To hit—that is, ask for another card—we pick up our original cards and scrape the edges on the felt surface toward us. This is the universal signal for a hit in all casinos that deal cards face down. The dealer will give you another card from the top of the stock he's holding in his hand.

If we want another card after our original hit, we scrape again. Simple as that. If we're satisfied with our hand, we slide the cards under our bet chips, and don't touch either the cards or the chips again.

As you may have noticed, no verbal commands are given to the dealer. The whole game can be played silently with these signals.

Single Deck

Hitting

Standing

Hitting and Standing in Multiple Deck Games

When all the players' cards are dealt *face up*, which is the usual case in multiple deck games involving four or more decks, there are different signals used by players when they wish to hit or stand.

If a player wants to draw another card, his signal for a hit is to point his index finger at the cards. Another card will be given to him by the dealer. Or the player may scratch the felt surface of the table behind his cards with his index finger, and this is also a signal for a hit. Either signal is universally accepted in American casinos.

If that same player wants to stand with his total, he simply waves his hand over the cards, with the palm face down, and the dealer will respect this signal and pass him by.

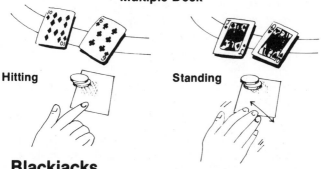

Multiple Deck

Hitting

Standing

Blackjacks

If a player is fortunate enough to be dealt a black-jack, which is an ace and 10-value card dealt to him as an original hand, he also turns these over immediately. But now for the good news. If the dealer doesn't have a blackjack also, the player will be paid off at once at 3-2, and his cards will be taken out of play.

Dealer's Upcard

In single deck games, if the dealer's upcard is a 10 (or 10-value), he immediately peeks at his hole card (the face down card below the upcard) to see if he has a blackjack. If he does, he turns the ace over and collects bets from all players who themselves don't have blackjacks. If he doesn't have an ace in the hole, he continues dealing the game.

If the dealer has an ace as an upcard, then he will ask the players if they want *insurance*. We'll go into this later.

Playing the Hand

Let's assume, in our theoretical game at the table

with the other two players, that the dealer's upcard is a 9. He doesn't have to peek at his hole card, for there's no way he can have a blackjack with a 9 showing.

The first baseman is the first to act on his hand. Remember, the players act first—that is, hit or stand—and then the dealer acts last, after all the players have made their decisions.

The first baseman scrapes his cards for a hit. He is dealt a queen. He scrapes the cards again for another hit, and gets a 7. Disgustedly, he turns over the cards he has been holding. He had a 3 and a 2, making his original hand a 5; with the queen and 7 he now holds 22, and has busted. The dealer takes away the first baseman's chips and cards and now turns his attention to the second player.

This player scrapes for a hit, gets a 4, and then happily slides his cards under his chips, a signal that he is now standing on his total. The dealer now turns to us. We look at our cards and find we hold a jack and a 9. Our 19 is a strong total, so we stand by—sliding the cards under our chips. Now it's the dealer's turn. He turns over his hole card.

His hole card was a 3, giving him a total of 12. Under the rules of the game, he must hit this hand, since it totals less than 17. He takes a card for himself by putting the top card of the stock face up next to his two original cards. It is a 4, giving him a 16. He must hit again. He has no options. His next card is a king. The dealer has gone over 21 and busted.

At this point, he takes the second player's original cards from under the chips and turns them over. This player had a 10 and a 6 for a 16, and drew the 4, giving him a 20. He is paid off at even-money. We are also paid off at even-money. It really didn't matter what totals either we or the second baseman had at this point, since the dealer busted and automatically lost.

After all the discards are put away, another round of play begins. Again, we all get two cards, and the dealer's upcard this time is a jack. Therefore, he peeks at his hole card, and when he finds he doesn't have a blackjack, he now turns toward the first baseman and the game goes on as before.

After a few rounds of play, even though there are cards left in the stock the dealer is holding, he'll shuffle up the cards. This is done to prevent card counters, experts who keep track of played out cards, from having an advantage over the house by knowing just what cards are left in the stock and betting accordingly.

Multiple Deck Games

By multiple deck games, we are referring to all games which use more than one deck.

When 4 or more decks are used, they're dealt from a **shoe**, a rectangular box which permits the cards to be slid out one at a time.

Double Deck Games

When two decks are used, these are still hand-held and all signals used by players are the same as in a single deck game. There are relatively few double deck games in comparison with either single or four and six deck games.

Splitting Pairs

Doubling Down

V. The Player's Options

Splitting Pairs

A player may split any matching cards of the same rank (pairs) if dealt as an original hand. For example, if he or she is dealt two 8s, these may be split. When pairs are split, they are turned over by the player if dealt face down; or separated, if dealt face up. Then a bet equal to the original bet is placed on the newly split card.

For example, if a player had bet $5, and received two 8s, and split them, then an additional $5 bet will be placed on the separated (split) 8. In essence, the player will now be betting on and playing out two hands.

He draws cards on the first 8 till he is satisfied with that total, and then he draws cards to the second 8, just as though this was an original hand.

Any pairs can be split, and for purposes of pairs, all 10-value cards are considered pairs. For example, a 10 and queen, or a jack and king, are considered pairs, but as we shall see, 10s should not be split.

Aces may be split, but unlike all other pairs, only one additional card will be dealt to each ace. Nevertheless, aces equal 11 and they should always be split.

Doubling Down

A player may double his bet on his original hand, at his option. When he does this, he will receive an additional card, and *one card* only. Therefore, it's important to remember that after doubling down, you can't stand on your original hand's total; you're going to be given an additional card by the dealer.

In practically all casinos except for the Northern Nevada ones, the rules permit doubling down on any two-card total. In Northern Nevada, only 10s and 11s may be doubled down.

When doubling down, a player turns over his cards if dealt face down, and puts out a bet equal to the original bet. When the cards have been dealt face up, he simply puts out an additional bet.

Surrender

In a few casinos, the player is allowed to forfeit half his original bet if he or she doesn't want to play the hand against the dealer. This is called **surrender.**

For example, suppose a player has a big bet out and the dealer shows a 10 as his upcard. The player has been dealt a 16, and feels that if he hits the hand, he'll bust, and if he stands, the dealer will have a 17 or more to beat him anyway. So, in those casinos allowing surrender, this player may surrender his hand. It's one of the few instances in which a verbal statement of the player's intent is made. He says *"Surrender,"* and the dealer will remove his cards and half his bet.

Insurance

When the dealer's upcard is an ace, before he peeks at his hole card the players are given the opportunity to *insure* their bets. The dealer will ask "Insurance?" and the players may bet up to one-half of their original bet that the dealer has a 10-value card in the hole.

If the dealer has a blackjack, the insurance bet wins, and is paid off at 2-1, but the original bet loses, and so, in essence, it's a standoff.

Therefore, an insurance bet is really a wager that the dealer has a blackjack. If he has one, the bet wins. If he doesn't have a 10-value card in the hole, the insurance bet is immediately lost and taken away and the game continues.

For example, if a player had a $10 bet out and then made a $5 insurance bet and the dealer didn't have a blackjack, the $5 bet would be taken away by the dealer. However, the game would now continue and the original $10 bet is still valid.

If the dealer in the above instance had a blackjack, he'd take away the player's original $10 bet and then pay $10, at 2-1 on the $5 insurance bet. In essence, it's a push.

VI. Winning Basic Strategies

Now we come to the chapter that will show you how to win at blackjack, using correct basic strategies.

Hitting and Standing Strategy

We'll divide this strategy into hard and soft totals. Remember, a hard hand is any one that doesn't contain an ace, or where an ace is counted as a 1 and not an 11.

For our considerations, all hard hands will begin with a total of 12. Hands below that total can be hit without worrying about busting.

Whether to hit or stand on any hand depends on two factors: the player's total and the dealer's upcard.

The following table will show the correct hitting and standing basic strategies:

Chart 1
Hitting and Standing—Hard Totals

	2	3	4	5	6	7	8	9	10	A
11 or less	H	H	H	H	H	H	H	H	H	H
12	H	H	S	S	S	H	H	H	H	H
13	S	S	S	S	S	H	H	H	H	H
14	S	S	S	S	S	H	H	H	H	H
15	S	S	S	S	S	H	H	H	H	H
16	S	S	S	S	S	H	H	H	H	H
17-21	S	S	S	S	S	S	S	S	S	S

H = Hit   S = Stand

Whenever the dealer shows a 7 or higher upcard (8, 9, 10 or ace), we assume that he already has a total of 17 and must stand with that total. Of course, that's not always the case, but it happens frequently enough for us to try and improve our total if it's below 17.

That's why we hit all hands from 12 through 16 when the dealer shows a 7, 8, 9, 10 or ace.

When the dealer shows a *bust* or *stiff* card, a 2, 3, 4, 5, or 6, we stand on all totals, except a hard 12 against a dealer's 2 or 3.

The reason we hit a 12 against a dealer's 2 or 3 upcard is that there are relatively fewer cards to bust our (and the dealer's) hand in that situation. Other than a 12 against the 2 and 3, we stand on all other totals when the dealer shows a stiff card. Our strategy in this regard is to force the dealer to hit his stiff hand and bust it, while we still have a valid hand.

It may be hard to memorize the table, but if you play out and practice some hands at home looking at the hitting and standing table, it will become easier to understand. And if you see the reasoning behind it, it's easier still.

Of course, we never hit a hard 17 or higher total, no matter what the dealer shows. The odds are very strong that we'll bust, and if our total is 19 or better we're favored to win by standing.

What we don't want to do is hit stiff totals from 12 to 16 when the dealer shows a 4, 5 or 6. These are the worst cards the dear can have (and the best for us to see as upcards) because he's most likely to bust his hand with those upcards.

And it would be foolish of us to bust first, when the dealer has such a good chance of busting and losing.

Hitting and Standing with Soft Totals

A **soft total** is any hand that contains an ace which is counted as 11 points. Thus, an ace-6 is a soft 17. There will be two tables here - the first is to be used in all jurisdictions other than Northern Nevada, for only hard 10s and 11s can be doubled down there.

Single and Multiple Deck Strategy Charts

The following charts and discussions present the best play for single and multiple deck blackjack games. In single deck games, play strategy as shown in chart. In multiple deck games, an asterisk (*) in the strategy chart indicates you should hit - do not double or split as in single deck play.

The full strategy charts on pages 40 and 41 show complete charts for single and multiple deck play respectively.

Chart 2
Hitting, Standing or Doubling Down with Soft Totals

	2	3	4	5	6	7	8	9	10	A
A2-A3	H	H	D*	D	D	H	H	H	H	H
A4-A5	H	H	D	D	D	H	H	H	H	H
A6	D*	D	D	D	D	H	H	H	H	H
A7	S	D	D	D	D	S	S	H	H	S
A8	S	S	S	S	S	S	S	S	S	S
A9	S	S	S	S	S	S	S	S	S	S

H = Hit   S = Stand   D = Double

All soft totals of 17 or below should be hit or doubled down. When the dealer shows a 4, 5 or 6, these soft totals will be doubled down. (Note that in a multiple deck game, A2 and A3 will be hit against the dealer's 4.)

The ace-6, the soft 17, will ***never be stood upon***. It will either be hit, or doubled down. When you see a player standing with a soft 17, you'll know he's very weak, and a loser.

The soft 19 and 20 are very strong and you should be content to stand with these totals. But the soft 18 is the tricky one. It is hit against the dealer's 9 and 10 upcard, and doubled down when the dealer holds the 3 through the 6. Practice these hands, and it will come naturally to you after a while.

The next table is for use only in Northern Nevada or any other jurisdiction where soft doubling down is not permitted.

Chart 3
Hitting and Standing with Soft Totals

	2	3	4	5	6	7	8	9	10	A
A2-A6	H	H	H	H	H	H	H	H	H	H
A7	S	S	S	S	S	S	S	H	H	S
A8-A9	S	S	S	S	S	S	S	S	S	S

H = Hit   S = Stand

As we see from the above table, we *always hit* the soft 17, and hit the soft 18 against the dealer's 9 or 10. These are important rules to remember, as well as standing on soft 19 or 20.

Doubling Down Strategies

The next table shows doubling down strategies, which correctly followed, give the player a tremendous edge over the casino. This table covers only hard doubling down totals, since the soft ones have already been covered in the previous section.

In Northern Nevada, where only a hard 10 or 11 can be doubled down, use the lines showing the 10 and 11.

Chart 4
Doubling Down with Hard Totals

	2	3	4	5	6	7	8	9	10	A
8(5-3,4-4)				D*	D*					
9	D*	D	D	D	D					
10	D	D	D	D	D	D	D	D		
11	D	D	D	D	D	D	D	D	D	D*

D = Double Down   **Blank = Do Not Double Down**

From this table we see that we **never** double down with a hard total of less than 8. Be sure to double down when you hold an 11. Many players are afraid to double down against a dealer's 10, but if you get a 10-value card on the 11, you have a 21, and can't lose.

If playing in Atlantic City, or in a casino where the dealer doesn't look at his hole card till all the players have acted upon their hands, the same double down rules apply. If the dealer finds he has a blackjack, the extra double down wager will be returned. The same holds true when splitting pairs. Only the original bet is lost.

Splitting Pairs

As we know, a player has the option of splitting any paired cards from his original hand, such as 3-3, 8-8, 9-9 and so forth. And all 10-value cards are considered pairs, such as jack-king, or 10-queen. The following chart shows correct splitting strategies. Split only those pairs shown on the chart.

Chart 5
Splitting Pairs

	2	3	4	5	6	7	8	9	10	A
22		Spl.*	Spl.	Spl.	Spl.	Spl.				
33			Spl.	Spl.	Spl.	Spl.				
66	Spl.*	Spl.	Spl.	Spl.	Spl.					
77	Spl.	Spl.	Spl.	Spl.	Spl.	Spl.				
88	Spl.	Spl.	Spl.	Spl.	Spl.	Spl.	Spl.	Spl.	Spl.	Spl.
99	Spl.	Spl.	Spl.	Spl.	Spl.		Spl.	Spl.		
AA	Spl.	Spl.	Spl.	Spl.	Spl.	Spl.	Spl.	Spl.	Spl.	Spl.

Spl. = Split   **Blank = Do Not Split**

Do not split 44, 55, 10s
Always split 88, AA

Be sure to split 8s and aces. A pair of 8s add up to 16, the worst stiff total a player can have, while 8s separately will form the base for a much stronger hand.

And aces should be split, because each ace adds up to 11, and a 10-value card drawn to that 11 is a powerful 21.

On the other hand, never split 4s and 5s. Two 4s add up to 8, while an individual 4 can end up as a stiff hand and a bad one at that. The 5s together add up to 10, and in most situations will be a doubled down hand. An individual 5 will usually lead to a stiff or a busted hand.

Don't split 10s (any 10-value pairs). These add up to 20, usually a winning hand. Splitting 10s is a bad move, and only the weakest players make it.

Some players will split any pair, no matter what the

dealer's upcard, thinking this is correct. But it isn't, and will end up costing the player money. Stick to our pair splits and you'll come out a winner. They all make sense.

For example, we don't split 7s against an 8 because if the player gets two 10-value cards, one on each 7, he'll still have only 17 and the dealer might already have an 18. And we don't split 9s against a dealer's 7 because two 9s add up to an 18, and the dealer might only have a 17. And we split 9s against the 8 because the 18 might only be a push, whereas a 10-value card on a 9 makes it a winner.

Resplitting Pairs

If an original pair should be split, then subsequent cards of the same rank should also be split. For example, suppose the dealer shows a 6 as his upcard, and you have a pair of 8s. You split the 8s, and get a 5 on the first 8 for a 13. Now you must stand on that hand because the *Hitting and Standing Strategies* call for no further cards to be drawn.

On the second 8, you're dealt another 8. This should be split and another bet put out. The rule is: resplit pairs where the first split is correct. Not all casinos allow resplitting. For example, aces generally can't be resplit. All other pairs can be re-split in practically all casinos except in Atlantic City.

Insurance

Whenever the dealer shows an ace as his upcard, he'll ask if any player wants insurance. As explained before, the insurance bet is a bet that the dealer *has* a

10-value card in the hole and thus has a blackjack.

In most cases, it's a bad bet. Don't take insurance unless you're familiar with an advanced card counting system.

Surrender

This is allowed in some casinos, where a player may forfeit half his bet and decide not to play his or her original hand against the dealer.

When you have the chance to surrender, stick to the following rules: surrender 15s and 16s against a dealer's 10, and a 16 against a dealer's ace. (Do not surrender 8-8-split it.)

In a multiple deck game, but not a single deck one, also surrender 16s (but not 88) against the dealer's 9.

Otherwise, don't surrender.

Doubling After Splitting Allowed

Some casinos permit the player to double down after splitting. Thus, if two eights were split, and a three was drawn to the first eight, this hand could be doubled by the player.

Thus, we'll split more aggressively when this rule is in effect. When this option is allowed, play your pairs as follows:

Player's Hand		Dealer's Upcard
22, 33, 77	split vs.	2-7
44	split vs.	5-6
66	split vs.	2-6

Chart 6
Single Deck Master Chart

	2	3	4	5	6	7	8	9	10	A
7/less	H	H	H	H	H	H	H	H	H	H
62	H	H	H	H	H	H	H	H	H	H
44/53	H	H	H	D	D	H	H	H	H	H
9	D	D	D	D	D	H	H	H	H	H
10	D	D	D	D	D	D	D	D	H	H
11	D	D	D	D	D	D	D	D	D	D
12	H	H	S	S	S	H	H	H	H	H
13	S	S	S	S	S	H	H	H	H	H
14	S	S	S	S	S	H	H	H	H	H
15	S	S	S	S	S	H	H	H	H	H
16	S	S	S	S	S	H	H	H	H	H
A2	H	H	D	D	D	H	H	H	H	H
A3	H	H	D	D	D	H	H	H	H	H
A4	H	H	D	D	D	H	H	H	H	H
A5	H	H	D	D	D	H	H	H	H	H
A6	D	D	D	D	D	H	H	H	H	H
A7	S	D	D	D	D	S	S	H	H	S
A8	S	S	S	S	S	S	S	S	S	S
A9	S	S	S	S	S	S	S	S	S	S
22	H	spl	spl	spl	spl	spl	H	H	H	H
33	H	H	spl	spl	spl	spl	H	H	H	H
66	spl	spl	spl	spl	spl	H	H	H	H	H
77	spl	spl	spl	spl	spl	spl	H	H	H	H
88	spl	spl	spl	spl	spl	spl	spl	spl	spl	spl
99	spl	spl	spl	spl	spl	S		spl	spl	S	S
AA	spl	spl	spl	spl	spl	spl	spl	spl	spl	spl

In Northern Nevada and other jurisdictions where doubling is restricted, usually to 10 and 11, hit instead of doubling down on all hands where "D" is indicated, except on A7, where you should stand.

Chart 7
Multiple Deck Master Chart

	2	3	4	5	6	7	8	9	10	A
7/less	H	H	H	H	H	H	H	H	H	H
62	H	H	H	H	H	H	H	H	H	H
44/53	H	H	H	H	H	H	H	H	H	H
9	H	D	D	D	D	H	H	H	H	H
10	D	D	D	D	D	D	D	D	H	H
11	D	D	D	D	D	D	D	D	D	H
12	H	H	S	S	S	H	H	H	H	H
13	S	S	S	S	S	H	H	H	H	H
14	S	S	S	S	S	H	H	H	H	H
15	S	S	S	S	S	H	H	H	H	H
16	S	S	S	S	S	H	H	H	H	H
A2	H	H	H	D	D	H	H	H	H	H
A3	H	H	H	D	D	H	H	H	H	H
A4	H	H	D	D	D	H	H	H	H	H
A5	H	H	D	D	D	H	H	H	H	H
A6	H	D	D	D	D	H	H	H	H	H
A7	S	D	D	D	D	S	S	H	H	S
A8	S	S	S	S	S	S	S	S	S	S
A9	S	S	S	S	S	S	S	S	S	S
22	H	H	spl	spl	spl	spl	H	H	H	H
33	H	H	spl	spl	spl	spl	H	H	H	H
66	H	spl	spl	spl	spl	H	H	H	H	H
77	spl	spl	spl	spl	spl	spl	H	H	H	H
88	spl	spl	spl	spl	spl	spl	spl	spl	spl	spl
99	spl	spl	spl	spl	spl	S	spl	spl	S	S
AA	spl	spl	spl	spl	spl	spl	spl	spl	spl	spl

In Northern Nevada and other jurisdictions where doubling is restricted, usually to 10 and 11, hit instead of doubling down on all hands where "D" is indicated, except on A7, where you should stand.

Multiple Deck Variations

The strategies for single and multiple deck blackjack (2 or more decks) differ only slightly, but we've presented them here so you can play winning blackjack in all situations.

Except for the following changes, single and multiple deck play is identical. In a multiple deck game:

Hit the following hands - do not double:

Player's Action		Dealer's Upcard
Hit 8	vs.	5 or 6
Hit 9	vs.	2
Hit 11	vs.	Ace
Hit A2 and A3	vs.	4
Hit A6	vs.	2

Hit the following hands - do not split:

Player's Action		Dealer's Upcard
Hit 22	vs.	3
Hit 66	vs.	2

VII. Card Counting and Money Management

Card Counting

Card counting, or keeping track of the cards already played out, is used by experts to beat the casino, and many of these experts have been barred from play.

This guidebook is not going to deal with card counting, other than to state that when a high proportion of 10-value cards and aces have been dealt out, the deck is unfavorable for the player. On the other hand, many smaller cards, such as 2s, 3s, 4s, 5s, 6s and 7s have been dealt out, the deck or decks are favorable for the player.

By watching the game closely, a player can get a good idea of the cards already dealt. For example, if on the first round of play in a single deck game, a disproportionate number of aces and 10s were dealt, then the deck is unfavorable. If a whole group of smaller cards showed on the opening round, with few aces or tens, then the deck is favorable.

A good rule in a single deck game only is to raise the bet when the first round showed a high proportion of small cards dealt out, and to lower the bet when this round showed a higher proportion of tens and aces.

With each round that follows, you see that cumulatively, more tens than normal have been dealt, keep your bet low. On the other hand, when you notice more small cards have been played out, raise your bet. This strategy works because a single deck is sensitive to changes in deck composition.

To effectively beat the casinos, whether playing a single or multiple deck game, we highly recommend that you learn a card counting strategy.

See back page for information on the Cardoza Base Count Strategy; the most effective card counting strategy ever produced for the average player. It is simple to learn yet extremely powerful. It will give any reader of this book a winning edge over the casino with just a few hours practice at home.

Money Management

Blackjack games can be like rollercoasters, with large winning and losing swings during the course of play. Don't get discouraged by these swings, because correct play will make you a winner in the long run.

As a rule of thumb, multiply your normal bet by 40 to determine how much to put on the table for one session of play. If you're betting $2 at a time, $80 will be sufficient. With $5 bets, about $200 will be needed. You can even hedge and take less, about $50 for $2 bets and $100 for $5 bets, but that's cutting it a little too thin.

Remember, play only with money you can afford to lose, that won't affect you financially and/or emotionally. Try to double your stake at the table. If you do, leave at once. You've done well. Or, if the table is choppy, and you're ahead, endeavor to leave a winner.

If you're losing, don't lose more than you bring to the table. Set a loss limit, and never reach into your pocket for more money. The first loss is the cheapest.

Money management can be as important as good play. Keep control of your emotions and your money, and you'll be a winner.

Leaving the Table When Ahead

When you're ahead, it's important to leave the table a winner.

There's nothing more wearying than being a big winner, and staying too long, watching the cards run from hot to cold and losing back all the money you've won, and then, worse, finding you end up a loser.

I developed a strong and enduring strategy to prevent this. I set aside my winnings carefully, so that I always knew just how much I was ahead.

Players are always counting their chips at the table, so it wasn't difficult to know just where I stood when the dealer was shuffling up the cards.

I did something else. I didn't spend too much time

at any table. I never played for more than an hour, and most times, less than that.

Since I was now card counting, I didn't want casino heat or the threat of being barred at a game I could win at. In other words, I didn't want the floormen and pit bosses to scrutinize my play.

I found the best way to stop them from doing this was to hit and run, not staying for hours at a time, giving them a chance to study my moves.

If I was ahead, I made certain to stay ahead. If I increased my stake to the point where I had doubled it, I found it best to leave right then and there, glancing at my watch and mumbling something about lunch or dinner, no matter what time it was. Or I'd ask the dealer where the nearest phone was, and gather up my chips and leave.

Once you know the game and want to play like a pro, it is strongly suggested that you buy the advanced strategies at the end of this book. They cover all you need to beat the casinos, no matter what kind of game you face, be it single or multiple deck games.

And with the mathematical advantage over the casino, the more you play, the more you can expect to win!

VIII. Riding a Winning Streak

As we have shown, the player has many options, but the dealer has none at all. He or she must adhere to the rules of the particular casino where the game is taking place. This definitely is an advantage to the player.

Here's one way to take advantage of this situation.

Sometimes, no matter how well you play, the cards run badly. When you get a 20, the dealer will get a 21, when you hold a blackjack, the dealer will turn over an immediate blackjack with a 10 on top. This happens.

Luck runs hot and luck runs cold, but in the end it evens out, while skill is always a constant factor.

Don't get discouraged by losses at a table. If you play correctly, in the long run, you'll end up as a winner. Nobody wins all the time, and good players won't lose all the time either. In the end, a player who knows what he or she is doing will wind up with more money than the original bankroll.

We mentioned a bad run of luck. There are times, however, when the opposite is true, when you'll get a disproportionate number of blackjacks, when everything will be running your way.

When this happens, it's wise to take advantage of the situation. Players call this a rush, and when you have that rush, try and make as much money as you can. Let me illustrate with a true story.

Building Up the Bankroll

When I first learned the game, I'd play for low stakes so that if I made a mistake at the table, it wouldn't cost me much. I started with $2 games in the downtown Las Vegas casinos, where small games were easier to come by than in the more opulent Strip casinos.

After I practiced for hours at a time, and had played for many hours, I felt comfortable with my game. I found I was making all the right moves, and rarely made a mistake.

I found also that I was slowly but surely increasing my bankroll, and winning more than I was losing, which gave me not only confidence, but the incentive to play at a bigger game.

It seemed like a big move in those faraway days to go from a $2 to a $5 table. At the $2 tables there were a number of poor players who didn't know much about the game and who hoped for a lucky streak to carry them over. At the $5 tables there still were a bunch of amateurs but there seemed to be always a few good players, card counters and would-be-pros.

I played the same way at the $5 tables that I had played in the smaller games, and found I was having the same results. I was slowly but surely increasing my blackjack bankroll.

There were times when I'd have a bad streak, or when the cards were unlucky for me, but I had conditioned myself to strict money management.

I limited my losses and never reached in my pocket for more money when I lost my table stake, and this made a big difference. My losses were small and I had some big wins, but I felt I could win more during these good streaks. The question was, how to do it?

Increasing Winnings

I decided that, when I had a good streak, when I increased my winnings at the table by 50%, I would take a shot and increase my minimum bets.

At the time, I was starting with two chips, two $5 chips as my opening bet on the first round of play just after the cards were shuffled and were about to be dealt. I was counting cards, keeping track of the large cards, the 10s, and the aces.

When the deck still held most of them after the first round of play, I increased my bet; when these large cards were depleted, I'd lower my bet. It was the same thing I had done at the $2 tables, except I was playing with $5 chips instead of $1 chips.

I was starting play with $200, and now I made up my mind that if I reached $100 in winnings, I'd increase my opening bet to three chips instead of two, and if the 10s and Aces were in the deck, I'd raise my bet to $30 instead of $20, as I had done before when my first bet was $10.

However, if the 10s and aces were being used up rapidly, I still reduced my bet to the minimum of one $5 chip. I wasn't going to fight the cards and just count on luck. I played at several tables the following week and had some good luck, winning more than I had lost, but I didn't really have a good streak where I was ahead $100. I would win $50 and $60, once $90, and my losses were small. I was, as usual, building up my bankroll slowly.

Then I found myself at a table where the only seat open was the anchor seat. Each of the other three players were betting at least $30 at a time, and a couple of them were playing two hands at once. They were all drinking heavily, and seemed to know each other.

They were holding their own, as far as I could tell, and none of them really knew how to play. This was easily apparent to me, when one player stood on an Ace and 6, a hand that should either be hit or doubled down in Vegas. Another didn't split 9s against a dealer's 6.

Well, that was their business. I felt if they really knew how to play they would have been big winners.

I started with my usual $10 bet as the cards were reshuffled and a cocktail waitress came around and asked if I wanted to have a drink. I shook my head.

I always wanted a clear head when playing blackjack. It's not just a game of luck; it's a game of skill and you must be alert at all times. The other players all had refills of Scotch and gin and vodka drinks. They were also all smokers and smoke covered the table like a small cloud.

The cards were dealt, the dealer showed a 5, and I got an Ace 6. I doubled down my soft 17 and won.

And kept on winning. It took me just a short while to be ahead $100. The decks retained the 10s and aces, and while I was winning, the others were still breaking even.

I started to bet $15 at the outset of play, and still kept winning. I was soon ahead $200. I raised my opening bet to $20. I could do nothing wrong.

Winning With Correct Strategy

On the first hand I was dealt two 8s against the dealer's 10. The correct play, I knew was to split them. One always splits 8s no matter what the dealer's upcard is.

As I did this, the player next to me, who was more than a little drunk, whispered "good luck," to me. Then he added, "that's a bad play, partner."

I shrugged my shoulders as if I half-agreed with him. But I wasn't going to play hunches; correct play had always worked out for me. The dealer turned over another 8 to go with my two 8s.

The rule is, if the first split is correct, all subsequent splits are correct. So I placed another $20 out on the table, and could see, through my peripheral vision, the others at the table shaking their heads in dismay at my so-called stupid play.

In rapid-fire dealing, I was given three 10s, so I held three 18s against the dealer's 10. He turned over his card to reveal a 6 underneath, and then dealt himself an ace for a 17.

So I won all three bets. Two of the other players at the table had stood on soft 17s, and one on a hard 16, so I was the only winner.

Just then a new dealer came on the scene and shuffled up the cards. I was now ahead $260, and still kept my $20 bet as I awaited the dealer's first cards. Soon I was ahead $300, and now decided to really go for big money.

My first bet was $25, and if the 10s and aces were in the deck, I was prepared to go to $50.

I rode that streak for another half-hour, and found myself up $550. I lost the $50 and called it quits, leaving with my biggest win ever till that time, $500!

Two weeks before I was playing at a $2 table and now I was making $50 bets!

Within two weeks, I moved to a $25 table and

have never looked back. What was important, how-ever, is that I took advantage of one of the player's big options, that of raising his bets whenever he faced favorable situations.

Even though I raised my bets, I still had the sense to lower the bets when the cards were poor in 10s and aces. And it worked wonders for my bankroll.

As I continued to play, I studied computer runs and developed the style of play that is revealed in the advanced strategies posted at the end of this book.

I not only played correctly at all times, but now had such a powerful card counting method, that the casino was helpless against my frequent onslaughts.

IX. A Final Winning Word

The most important word to remember is patience. If you play serious blackjack, you'll have an advantage over the house, but it's a small advantage.

But that small advantage can make a lot of money for you, if you increase your bets at appropriate times and lower them at other times.

We mentioned **riding the rush**, making the most when the cards are running well.

Also, remember to be patient. If you've won a few hands in a row, but now all the 10s and aces are depleted, lower your bet. Don't count on luck. Wait for the cards to turn favorable again.

If you're losing, as will sometimes happen, don't

ever increase your bets in the hope of winning back your losses with a couple of big bets. If you've been betting two chips at the outset, keep betting the two chips. Be patient.

Cards run in cycles and they will turn around in your favor. If they don't and you lose your table stake, then leave the table immediately. Controlling your emotions and your bankroll at the table is as important as playing correctly.

So, stay in control. Practice patience. Ride the good streaks and pull in your horns when the bad streaks come around.

In this way, you'll always be doing the right thing, and doing the right thing in blackjack means making money!

X. Glossary of Blackjack Terms

Anchorman—Also called **Third Baseman.** The player in the last seat or the player who acts upon his hand last at the table.

Blackjack—1. The name of the casino game; also known as "21." 2. An original hand consisting of an ace and 10-value card, paid off at 3-2 if held by a player.

Burning a Card—The removal of the top card by the dealer before dealing out cards on the first round of play.

Busting—Also known as **Breaking.** Drawing cards to a hand so that its total is 22 or more, a loser.

Card Counting—Keeping mental track of the cards played out to see if the deck is favorable or unfavorable.

Chips—The gambling tokens issued by the casino to take the place of cash, for betting purposes.

Dealer—The casino employee in charge of the blackjack game, who deals out cards and collects and pays off bets.

Deck—The standard pack of cards containing 52 cards of four suits.

Double Down—The doubling of an original bet by a player, who will then receive only one additional card.

Draw—See **Hit**.

Favorable Deck—A deck whose remaining cards are to the advantage of the player as far as probability of winning is concerned.

First Baseman—The player who receives cards and acts upon them first. Usually occupies the first end seat at the table.

Hand—The cards the players hold and act upon.

Hard Total—A hand containing no aces, or where the ace is counted as 1.

Hit—Also called **Draw**. The act of getting one or more cards for the original hand.

Hole Card—The unseen dealer's card.

Insurance—A bet that can be made when a dealer shows an ace as an upcard. This bet wins if the dealer has a blackjack.

Multiple Deck—The use of more than one deck in the game of casino blackjack.

Natural—A term for a blackjack.

Push—A tie between the dealer and player, where no money changes hands. It's a standoff.

Round of Play—A complete cycle of play where all the players and the dealer act upon their hands.

Shoe—A device used when dealing four or more decks.

Shuffle, Shuffle Up—The mixing up of the cards by the dealer.

Single Deck Game—A game in which only one deck of cards is used.

Soft Total—A hand containing an ace that counts as 11 points. Example, an ace-9 is a soft 20 total.

Splitting Pairs—The separation of two cards of equal rank, such as 8s, so that they're played as two separate hands.

Standing, Standing Pat—Not hitting a hand.

Stiff Hand—Any hand that may bust if drawn to, such as a hard 12-16.

Ten-Value Card—The 10, jack, queen or king, all valued at ten points.

Third Baseman—See **Anchorman**.

Tip or Toke—A gratuity given to or bet for the dealer by a player.

Twenty-One—Another name for the casino game of blackjack.

Upcard—The open card of the dealer which can be seen by the players prior to their acting on their hands.

AVERY CARDOZA'S CASINO CHAMPION
Get ready for the...
CASINO GAME OF A LIFETIME!
Incredible CD-ROM Windows Computer Casino Simulation
Absolutely Realistic Casino Play Against Your Computer!

Personally designed by Avery Cardoza and the **master game designers** at *Cardoza Entertainment*, this amazing state-of-the-art game took 15 months and **$375,000** to create. This **great experience** is coming to you in Fall 1995! You won't believe it until you see it, and play it, and experience it! Look for it in your software stores, or **call** Cardoza Publishing (718)743-5229 to order.

REALISM AND FULL CD-ROM CAPABILITIES IS THE KEY TO FUN
Realistic game-like simulation in first-person true-perspective puts you right at the table and ***playing***. Challenge the casino in blackjack, craps, roulette, slots and video poker. Simulated dealers and players are **fully animated**; they talk, they offer advice, and scream and yell when they win; if you need advice, the on-line tutor, help feature and **free** Avery Cardoza book are there for you. **Surprises** await you at every table. What does that mean? - *Play the game and find out...*

Sensational Blackjack - Life-like 21 features single and multiple deck play, five built-in casino rules *and* customizable options, 3 dealers including the **Wild Man**; **actual** shuffling, dealing, betting *and* playing animations. Dealers **talk**, announce player totals, shuffle cards, react to actions, peek under hole cards for blackjack, look at each player in turn, **more**. Like regular casino blackjack - but more fun! All standard 21 features, multiple player spots, expert options, learning modes, more!

Terrific Craps - Make any bet you want and join the **excitement** at the craps table. Play the come, the odds, bet the field, take the niner, Big Six - **go for broke**. Roll the dice, hear the tumult of a hot table. Get caught up in it, the game is **real**!

Jackpot Slots - An enormous **variety** of machines gives you **non-stop play** and all sorts of possibilities to land the lucky **jackpot**! Three and five cylinder machines in many styles and payouts gives you **all the action** you can handle.

Skillful Video Poker - Test your skills against the **most realistic** video poker you've seen. Play Jacks or Better, flattop, Progressives, Deuces Wild, Joker Wild, more. What's the right move? Check Cardoza's expert **on-line advice** for hints.

Glamorous Roulette - With more than **150 possible bets** and combinations to choose from, the roulette player in you won't be able to quit -at least not 'til you **break the bank**! Work out your own systems, if they work here, *who knows*...

Also look for *Avery Cardoza's*
POKER CHAMPION & BLACKJACK CHAMPION
Distributed Nationally in software Stores, or call (718)743-5229

BEAT THE HOUSE™
THE ULTIMATE GAMING TUTOR AND SIMULATOR
(Available in Windows, DOS and Macintosh)

EXPERIENCE THE THRILL OF CASINO GAMING - With vividly detailed graphics and superior sound, *Beat The House* makes you part of the action! You'll experience the thrill of casino gaming and learn the skills and techniques of the professional gambler. Play for fun in the simulated casino environment, or play like a pro using the unique pop-up genius gaming tutor and Avery Cardoza's 160 page guide to winning (included free).

LEARN HOW TO PLAY AND WIN! - The pop-up tutor serves as **your personal gaming coach**. It analyzes every move and shows how to play each game **like a pro**. In **BLACKJACK**, you'll learn how to **optimize** your strategy and **count cards like a pro**; in **CRAPS**, learn how to **maximize your odds** in single or double odds games; in **VIDEO POKER**, you learn **what to hold** and when to draw; in **ROULETTE**, you'll learn money management as you try the more than **150 bets available**; and in **SLOTS**, you'll go for the big jackpot on **multiple payout or progressive machines**.

PLAY FOR FUN - Tired of playing by the rules? Turn off the coach and play with reckless abandon; forget money management, counting and strategies. Bet the farm and then some. Jump around from table to table and place those six-figure bets- why not?

MULTIPLE PLAYERS - One to four people can play against each other, or computer players will fill the empty seats to add excitement. Watch out though, computer players play to win!

FREE BONUS - Included free with the game is the *Beat the House Companion*, a strategy guide and tip book written specifically for *Beat the House* by gambling pro Avery Cardoza.

To order send just $49.95 (plus postage) by check or money order to:
  <u>Cardoza Publishing</u>, P.O. Box 1500, Cooper Station, New York, NY 10276

BEAT THE HOUSE™
THE ULTIMATE GAMING TUTOR AND SIMULATOR

Yes! Rush me **Beat the House**, the exciting new casino simulation game and the **free 160 page bonus**, **Beat the House Companion** by Avery Cardoza. Enclosed is a check or money order for $49.95 (plus postage and handling) made out to:

<u>Cardoza Publishing</u>, P.O. Box 1500, Cooper Station, New York, NY 10276
MC/VISA/AMEX orders by phone (718) 743 - 5229

Include $5.00 postage and handling for U.S. & Canada, other countries $10.00. Orders outside U.S., money order payable in U.S. dollars on U.S. bank only.

NAME _____ Disk Size _____

ADDRESS _____

CITY _____ STATE _____ ZIP _____

GRI BJ

Four Fun Handheld Casino Games!!

These **exciting palm-sized** games made by Saitek, *the world leader in intelligent electronic games* can be taken anywhere! They feature **superb sound effects** and **large LCD screens** to bring you the excitement and challenge of Las Vegas casino play!

SAITEK PRO BLACKJACK - $49.95

LAS VEGAS EXCITEMENT/LEARN TO WIN MONEY - Have fun and learn how to win at the same time with this great blackjack computer. This exciting device allows you to improve your skills so when you hit the real casino, you're prepared to be a winner. All the features of casino blackjack are included along with exciting options. **PACKED WITH FEATURES -** Choose any casino environment you want. Play against 1-6 deck games; choose any number of players at the table, one to four. You won't lose your shirt - bets between $10 and $1,000 are allowed. The built-in coach gives advice on all the options: hitting, standing, splitting, doubling down and insurance; and even introduces you to winning card counting methods!

SAITEK PRO VIDEO POKER - $49.95

Another fun and exciting winner from Saitek, this fast-paced, action-packed and easy-to-play game is difficult to put down. Play once and you're hooked forever! **TWO CHALLENGING GAMES IN ONE -** Test your skills against not only Jacks or Better Video Poker, but against Deuces Wild. **Random shuffling** action keeps the game **realistic** - just like in the casinos. Bet anywhere from one coin to five, and **play to win.** Go for the Royal Flush jackpot! **EXTRA FEATURES - Hold-Call** buttons; **Increase Bet** button for aggressive play; **Credit Button,** plus shows payoffs and probabilities for **every** winning hand.

SAITEK PRO POKER - $49.95

REALISTIC POKER CHALLENGE - Imagine, take your Friday night poker game with you! You bet, call, raise, fold and even bluff just as in real poker. But be careful, Cautious Clay, Mustang Mel and Dr. Wynne - the three real-life poker characters **built into the game** - play to win also. There's the cool, statistical player, the aggressive, bullying player and the cautious, conservative player. **IMPROVE YOUR GAME - Test your skills** against each opponents strategies and styles; the press of a button changes the players seats to keep you on your toes. **Extra features** such as *Hold-Call, Options, Hint* and *Credit Buttons* keep game realistic. *On-screen tutor* provides tips on better strategy.

Also **SAITEK PRO ROULETTE - $49.95**

FOUR GREAT CHALLENGING GAMES!

Yes! Enclosed is a check or money order for $49.95 for each game desired - buy one or buy all - plus postage and handling, made out to:
Cardoza Publishing, P.O. Box 1500, Cooper Station, New York, NY 10276
MC/VISA/AMEX orders by phone (718)743-5229
For U.S. and Canada, please include $5.00 postage and handling for first game, $1.00 extra for each additional game. Other countries $10.00 for first game, $2.00 for each additional one. Outside U.S.A, money order payable in U.S. dollars on U.S. bank only.
Circle desired item(s):   Blackjack   Video Poker   Poker   Roulette

NAME _____

ADDRESS _____

CITY _____ STATE _____ ZIP _____

GRI BJ

Win at Blackjack Without Counting Cards!
Breakthrough in Blackjack!!!
The Cardoza 1,2,3 Non-Counter Strategy

Beat Multiple Deck Blackjack Without Counting Cards!

You heard right! Now, for the **first time** ever, **win** at multiple deck black-jack **without counting cards**! Until I developed the Cardoza Multiple Deck Non-Counter (The 1,2,3 Strategy), I thought it was impossible. Don't be in-timidated anymore by 4, 6 or 8 deck games - for now you have the **advantage**!

Exciting Strategy - Anyone Can Win!

We're **excited** about this strategy for it allows anyone at all to **have the advantage** over any casino in the world in a multiple deck game. You don't need a great memory, you don't count cards, you don't need to be good at math - you only need to know the **winning secrets** of the Cardoza Multiple Deck Non-Counter and use but a **little effort** to be a **winner**.

Simple But Effective - Be a Leisurely Winner!

This strategy is so **simple**, yet so **effective**, you will be amazed. With a **minimum of effort**, this remarkable strategy, which we also call the 1,2,3 (as easy as 1,2,3), allows you to **win** without studiously following cards. Drink, converse, whatever - they'll never suspect that you can **beat the casino**!

Not as powerful as a card counting strategy, but **powerful enough to make you a winner** - with the odds!!!

Extra Bonus!

Complete listing of all options and variations at blackjack and how they affect the player. ($5 Value!) **Extra, Extra Bonus!!** Not really a bonus for we could not sell you the strategy without protecting you against gettting barred. The 1,000 word essay, "How to Disguise the Fact That You're an Expert," and 1,500 word "How Not To Get Barred," are also included free. ($15 Value)

To Order, send ~~$75~~ $50 by check or money order to <u>Cardoza Publishing</u>

- -

$25 OFF (Only $50 With This Coupon)

Please Rush Me the Cardoza Multiple Deck 1,2,3 Non-Counter!

Yes, I want to **be a winner** at blackjack. Please *rush* me the **Cardoza Multiple Deck Non-Counter (The 1,2,3 Strategy)**. I understand that the bonus essays and the "Options and Variations" Charts are included free! Enclosed is a check or money order for $50 (plus postage and handling) made out to: <u>Cardoza Publishing</u>, P.O. Box 1500, Cooper Station, New York, NY 10276

MC/VISA/AMEX orders by phone (718) 743-5229

Include $5.00 postage and handling for U.S. & Canada, other countries $10.00. Orders outside U.S., money order payable in U.S. dollars on U.S. bank only.

NAME _____

ADDRESS _____

CITY _____ STATE _____ ZIP _____

GRI BJ

Order Now! - 30 Day Money Back Guarantee!

Win Money at Blackjack! Special Introductory Offer!
THE CARDOZA BASE COUNT STRATEGY

Finally, a count strategy has been developed which allows the average player to play blackjack like a **pro**! The Cardoza Base Count Strategy has been used successfully by graduates of the Cardoza School of Blackjack for years. But **now**, for the **first time**, this "million dollar" strategy, which was only available previously to Cardoza students, is available to **you**!

FREE VACATIONS! A SECOND INCOME? - You bet! Once you learn this strategy, you will have the skills to **consistently win big money** at blackjack. The casino's bankroll is yours for the taking.

BECOME AN EXPERT IN TWO DAYS - Why struggle over complicated strategies that aren't as powerful? In just **two days or less**, you can learn the Cardoza Base Count and be among the best blackjack players. Friends will look up to you in awe - for you will be a **big winner** at blackjack.

BEAT ANY SINGLE OR MULTIPLE DECK GAME - We show you how, with just a **little effort**, you can effectively beat any single or multiple deck game.

You'll learn how to count cards, how to use advanced betting and playing strategies, how to make money on insurance bets, and much, much, more in this 6,000 word, chart-filled strategy package.

SIMPLE TO USE, EASY TO MASTER - You too can win! The **power** of the Cardoza Base Count strategy is not only in its **computer-proven** winning results but also in its **simplicity**. Many beginners who thought card counting was too difficult have given the Cardoza Base Count the acid test - they have **won consistently** in casinos around the world.

The Cardoza Base Count strategy is designed so that **any player** can win under practical casino conditions. **No need** for a mathematical mind or photographic memory. **No need** to be bogged down by calculations. Keep **only one number** in your head at any time.

BONUS! AND EXTRA BONUS!! - But to provide extra precautions, the fact-filled 1,500 word essay, "How Not to Get Barred," and the 1,000 word essay "How to Disguise the Fact that You're an Expert," are included **free**!!! You'll learn how to project a losing image, role playing, how pit bosses spot counters and other invaluable skills that will increase your profit potential.

To order, send $50 by check or money order to <u>Cardoza Publishing</u>

WIN MONEY AT BLACKJACK! MAIL THIS COUPON IN TODAY!
Yes, I want to **win big money** at blackjack. Please *rush* me the **Cardoza Base Count Strategy** package. Enclosed is a check or money order for $50 (plus postage and handling) made out to:

Cardoza Publishing, P.O. Box 1500, Cooper Station, New York, NY 10276
MC/VISA/AMEX orders by phone (718) 743 - 5229
Include $5.00 postage and handling for U.S. & Canada, other countries $10.00. Orders outside U.S., money order payable in U.S. dollars on U.S. bank only.

NAME _____

ADDRESS _____

CITY _____ STATE _____ ZIP _____

Order Now! - 30 Day Money Back Guarantee!   GRI BJ

63

CARDOZA SCHOOL OF BLACKJACK
- Home Instruction Course - $200 OFF! -

At last, after years of secrecy, the **previously unreleased** lesson plans, strategies and playing tactics formerly available only to members of the Cardoza School of Blackjack are now available - and at substantial savings. **Now,** you can **learn at home,** and at your own convenience. Like the full course given at the school, the home instruction course goes **step-by-step** over the winning concepts. We'll take you from layman to **pro.**

MASTER BLACKJACK - Learn what it takes to be a **master player.** Be a **powerhouse,** play with confidence, impunity, and **with the odds** on your side. Learn to be a **big winner** at blackjack.

MAXIMIZE WINNING SESSIONS - You'll **learn how** to take a good winning session and make a **blockbuster** out of it, but just as important, you'll learn to cut your losses. Learn exactly when to end a session. We cover everything from the psychological and emotional aspects of play to altered playing conditions (through the **eye of profitability**) to protection of big wins. The advice here could be worth **hundreds (or thousands) of dollars** in one session alone. Take our guidelines seriously.

ADVANCED STRATEGIES - You'll learn the **latest** in advanced winning strategies. Learn about the **ten-factor,** the **Ace-factor,** the effects of rules variations, how to protect against dealer blackjacks, the winning strategies for single and multiple deck games and how each affects you; you'll learn the **true count,** the multiple deck true count variations, and much, much more.

And, of course, you receive the full Base Count Strategy package.

$200 OFF - LIMITED OFFER - The Cardoza School of Blackjack home instruction course, a $295 retail value (or $895 if taken at the school) is available now for just $95!!!

BONUS! - Rush your order in **now,** for we're also including, **absolutely free,** the 1,000 word essays, "How to Disguise the Fact that You're an Expert", and "How Not to Get Barred". Among other **inside information** contained here, you'll learn about the psychology of pit bosses and how they spot counters.

To order, send $95 by check or money order to <u>Cardoza Publishing</u>:

SAVE $200 (regular $295 - Only $95 with coupon)

Order Now! Please rush me the Cardoza School of BJ Home instruction Course. Enclosed is a check or money order for $95 (plus postage) to :
<u>Cardoza Publishing</u>, P.O. Box 1500, Cooper Station, New York, NY 10276
MC/VISA/AMEX orders by phone (718)743 - 5229

Include $5.00 postage and handling for U.S. & Canada, other countries $10.00. Orders outside U.S., money order payable in U.S. dollars on U.S. bank only.

NAME _____

ADDRESS _____

CITY _____ STATE _____ ZIP _____

Order Now! - 30 Day Money Back Guarantee!   GRI BJ